Rubber Band Jewellery

Loom and Hook

Pam Leach

First published in 2014

Search Press Limited
Wellwood, North Farm Road,
Tunbridge Wells, Kent TN2 3DR

Text copyright © Pam Leach 2014

Photographs by Paul Bricknell at
Search Press Studios

Photographs and design copyright
© Search Press Ltd 2014

Print ISBN: 978-1-78221-190-7
EPUB ISBN: 978-1-78126-248-1
Mobi ISBN: 978-1-78126-249-8

Suppliers
If you have difficulty in obtaining any of the
materials and equipment mentioned in this book,
then please visit the Search Press website for
details of suppliers: www.searchpress.com

Printed in China

Contributors

It is practically impossible to be part of the
Beads Direct team and not be inspired to
make jewellery – I am fortunate to work with
some very talented people!
Everything that we do involves a team effort
but I would particularly like to thank
Laura Bajor for creating these fun designs.
On behalf of Beads Direct, I would also like
to thank Search Press for inviting us
to produce our second book for you.

Pam Leach

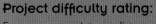

Project difficulty rating:

Easy	Intermediate	Advanced
★★★	★★★	★★★

Contents

Introduction

Who would have thought that such fabulous jewellery and accessories could be created from rubber bands!

You can create simple linked bracelets in a multitude of colours and wear them all together or add beads, charms or ribbon to really personalise your look. Using the loom will help you to make more complicated designs – just follow the instructions to make your favourites.

This fun new creative hobby has captured the imagination of both the young and not so young, and with new colours and textures of bands becoming available, the possibilities are endless – this trend is sure to continue.

Creating your own jewellery at any level is so enjoyable, great to do on your own, or share with your friends.

Have fun – you'll soon be hooked!

Pam Leach and the Beads Direct team

Tools and materials

Tools

You will need very few tools for making rubber band jewellery, all of which are readily available: a **hook** (very similar to a regular crochet hook) for making simple designs, and for use in conjunction with a loom; a **loom**, for making more complicated designs; and occasionally you will need **small jewellery pliers** to open jump rings. There are several different brands of loom available, but they all have a similar construction, so any of them will work with the designs in this book.

Materials

The main materials you will use are **rubber bands**. These are available in a huge array of different colours. You will also need **S-clips** to secure your designs and connect sections together; and you may need to use **jump rings** if you are attaching charms or pendants to your designs.

Adjusting the loom

You will often see an instruction at the beginning of a project telling you to "adjust the loom". In the photograph of the two looms (below), you will see that the loom on the left, which has not been adjusted, has its pegs all in straight lines, whereas the pegs of the loom on the right, which has been adjusted, make a pointed triangle shape at the bottom. Each column of pegs can be removed and repositioned, and some designs require the middle column to be moved downwards by one peg.

Each peg forms a C-shape, so when the instructions say the pegs are facing the left, or right, for example, it means the open side of the C-shape faces that way.

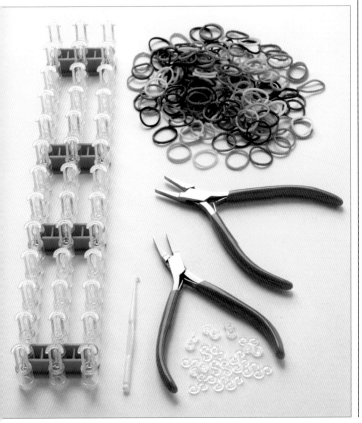

Techniques

Opening a jump ring

1 Using two small pairs of jewellery pliers, hold the jump ring securely, twisting one pair of pliers to the right and the other to the left to open the ring.

2 Attach the jump ring to the pendant or charm, and to the piece of rubber band jewellery, and reverse the process in step 1 to close the jump ring so that it forms a continuous ring again.

Threading a bead

Simply double a band and thread it through the hole in the bead so that the band is protruding from either side.

Doubling bands

You may need to double a band for some projects, and the band can either go over one peg (below left) or over two pegs (below right).

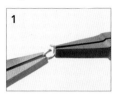

Trebling bands

Twist the band round the hook three times, and use the hook to help you stretch it over the peg.

Making a figure of 8

You can do this by pushing both index fingers through a band and twisting it.

Extending technique

Some projects require an extension to be made, for example, to a bracelet, and this is done by following the simple looping technique, as explained on the front flap. Begin looping extra bands through your design in the colour of your choice (below left) and when the extension is the correct length (below right) you can attach an S-clip to secure and finish it off.

Making a slip knot

This is useful for finishing off a design so it does not unravel.

1 Take a finishing band and pull it through all remaining bands of the design.

2 Pull the end of the band on your index finger over the end on the hook.

3 Pull the blue band into a knot to secure this end of the design.

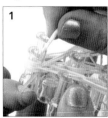

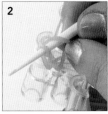

Simple Linked Bracelet ★★★

Materials:
25 x rubber bands (8 x hot pink,
    8 x orange, 9 x green)
1 x S-clip

Tools:
Hook

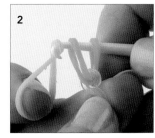

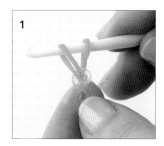

Instructions:

1 The basic looping technique, used to make this bracelet, can be done with a loom (see back flap) or just a hook, as shown here, and on the front flap. To begin, fold a green band onto the hook and attach an S-clip.

2 Now take an orange band and pull it through the loops of the green band with the hook, then place the hook through the other loop of the orange band.

3 Continue looping different coloured rubber bands in the three-colour pattern until the bracelet is long enough to fit your wrist; about 25 bands is enough for a medium-sized wrist.

4 Attach the last band to the other side of the S-clip to finish the bracelet. You can make single-coloured bracelets, or experiment with lots of colours and create your own unique look.

Bold and Basic

This linked bracelet is quick and easy to make and looks great worn in twos, threes or more with lots of contrasting colours.

Infinity Bracelet ★★★

Materials:

20 x rubber bands (10 x yellow
   and 10 x blue)

1 x purple infinity connector

1 x S-clip

Tools:

Hook

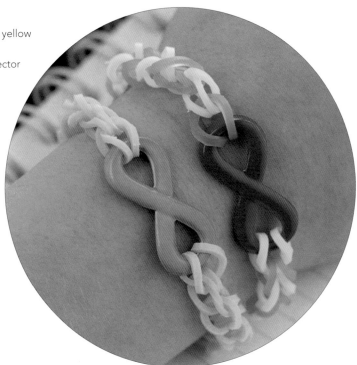

Instructions:

1 Loop a blue rubber band round the infinity connector and then loop a yellow band through this.

2 Continue by looping a further eight bands, using the basic looping technique (see front flap), with alternate blue and yellow bands.

3 Attach an S-clip to the last rubber band.

4 Repeat this process on the other side of the infinity connector, this time starting with a yellow rubber band. When you have finished looping all the bands, connect the last band to the other side of the S-clip to secure the bracelet.

Infinite Fun

For maximum impact, make your infinity bracelet in one colour or, if you prefer, you can alternate the colours to complement the shade of the infinity connector.

Tea Party Necklace ★★★

Materials:
100 x rubber bands (50 x
    yellow, 50 x orange)

1 x cupcake charm

1 x jump ring

1 x S-clip

Tools:
Hook

2 x small pair of pliers

Instructions:

1 Fold an orange band onto the hook and attach an S-clip.

2 Take a second orange band and pull it through the loops of the first band with the hook, then place the hook through the other loop of the second band.

3 Now repeat this process using two yellow bands.

4 Using the basic looping technique (see front flap), create a continuous necklace by alternating two orange bands and then two yellow bands – we have used 100 bands in total for this necklace, but you can adjust the number either to lengthen or shorten the necklace.

5 When you have looped all the bands, secure the last one to the other end of the S-clip to join the necklace.

6 Take the jump ring and open it as shown right, using two small pairs of jewellery pliers. Connect the cupcake charm to the centre of the necklace using the jump ring.

7 To finish the necklace, close the jump ring securely so that it forms a continuous ring again.

6

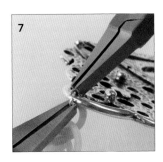

7

Party Piece
This fun necklace can be made with a variety of different charms and as many colours as you like. Make them for all your friends!

Super-cute Bag Charm ★★★

Materials:

18 x rubber bands (10 x
   yellow, 8 x green)

2 x S-clips

1 x lobster keyring clasp

1 x puppy dog charm

1 x paw print charm

Tools:

Hook

Instructions:

1 Thread the first yellow band through the metal loop on the puppy dog charm and connect an S-clip to the band.

2 Connect a yellow band to the lobster keyring clasp and, using the basic looping technique (see front flap), loop one more yellow band, then two green, two yellow, two green and one yellow band using the hook.

3 Attach the last band to the S-clip to connect the charm.

4 Repeat this process to connect the puppy paw print charm to the lobster keyring clasp.

Personal Charms

These charms can be hooked to bags, buttonholes and anywhere else you can think of. For a different look, use boy and girl charms with blue- and pink-coloured bands.

Woven Ribbon Bracelet ★★★

Materials:
25 x pink rubber bands

1 x S-clip

1 x 40cm length of 3mm
 purple satin ribbon

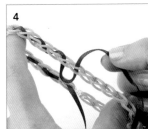

Tools:
Hook

Instructions:

1 Fold a pink band onto the hook and attach an S-clip. Using the basic looping technique (see front flap), loop 24 more bands with the hook.

2 Secure the last band to the other end of the S-clip to join the bracelet.

3 Take the ribbon and begin weaving it up and down through the loops of the bands, leaving approximately 10cm (4in) of ribbon at the start of the bracelet.

4 Stretch the bracelet between your thumb and index finger, so it opens up the rubber bands for ease of threading.

5 Once you have woven the ribbon through the length of the bracelet, tie a knot over the S-clip.

6 Then tie the ends of the ribbon in a pretty bow. Remember to leave a bit of slack in the ribbon so that you can get the bracelet on and off your wrist easily.

Simple and Cute

For a complementary look, make a second bracelet with lilac bands and two lengths of different-coloured ribbon to weave through the bands.

Linked Charm Bracelet ★★★

Materials:

25 x rubber bands (5 x yellow, 5 x green,
   5 x pink, 5 x orange, 5 x blue)

1 x S-clip

5 x jump rings

5 x charms of your choice

Tools:

Hook

2 x small pair of pliers

Instructions:

1 Fold a yellow band onto the hook and attach an S-clip. Using the basic looping technique (see front flap), loop four more yellow bands using the hook, then five each of the green, pink, orange and blue bands.

2 Secure the last blue band to the other end of the S-clip to join the bracelet.

3 Open a jump ring with the pliers (see page 7), and attach the charm to it.

4 Then attach the jump ring and charm to the bracelet by threading it through the fifth yellow band. Close the jump ring so it forms a continuous ring again.

5 Attach the rest of the charms to the bracelet in the same way to finish it off, taking care to space them evenly around the bracelet by attaching them to the fifth band of each colour.

3

4

Mix and Match
There are so many different charms available, you can make lots of these bracelets to match your outfits, using different themes and different band colours.

Finger Loop Bracelet ★★★

Materials:

For a bracelet: 44 x rubber
    bands (22 x orange, 22 x
    yellow)

1 x S-clip

For an anklet: 57 x rubber
    bands (38 x pink,
    19 x green)

1 x S-clip

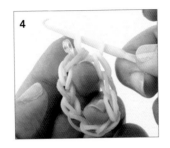

Tools:

Hook

Instructions:

1 Begin this bracelet by making the finger loop. Fold a yellow band onto the hook and attach an S-clip. Then, using alternate orange and yellow, loop nine more bands, using the basic loooping technique (see front flap).

2 Check that the ring will go around your finger, adding more bands if required.

3 Then slide the hook through the two loops of the orange band on the S-clip. You can now remove the S-clip, as all four loops are on the hook.

4 Connect a yellow band through all four loops that are on your hook by pulling the band through as normal.

5 Loop a further nine bands, continuing to alternate between orange and yellow. With the ring round your finger, check that length is sufficient to reach to your wrist. If not, add more bands to fit.

6 Now add 12 more bands and connect an S-clip to the last one. Count back 12 bands up this length and slide your hook through the band. Connect a new band and make 12 more loops for the other side of the wrist part of the design.

7 To finish, connect the last band to the other end of the S-clip.

8 To create the anklet, follow the pattern for the bracelet design, but use nine bands for the toe ring, 18 bands for the connecting piece and 30 bands to create the anklet. Check for fit as you work, and use more bands if necessary, alternating between two pink bands and one green.

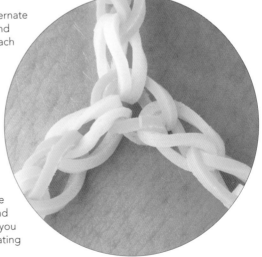

Fit to Size

It is so easy to make this bracelet and anklet larger or smaller – simply adjust the number of bands to fit your hand or foot. For the anklet, we have alternated two pink bands with one green band to produce an attractive pattern.

Double Band Ring ★★★

Materials:

22 x pink rubber bands

1 x S-clip

1 x silver slider charm bead
with crystal

Tools:

Hook

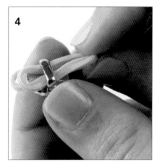

Instructions:

1 This design uses the basic looping technique (see front flap), but you will use two bands to form each loop instead of just one.

2 Fold two bands onto the hook and attach an S-clip.

3 Make four more loops with the twin pink bands so that you have five loops in total (but 10 bands).

4 Slide the charm bead onto two rubber bands so that it sits in the middle of them. Now loop this band into the design as normal.

5 Then make the next five loops and attach the last pair of bands to the other end of the S-clip to finish off the ring. If you need to use more bands, make sure you have an even number either side of the charm, so that the ring is symmetrical.

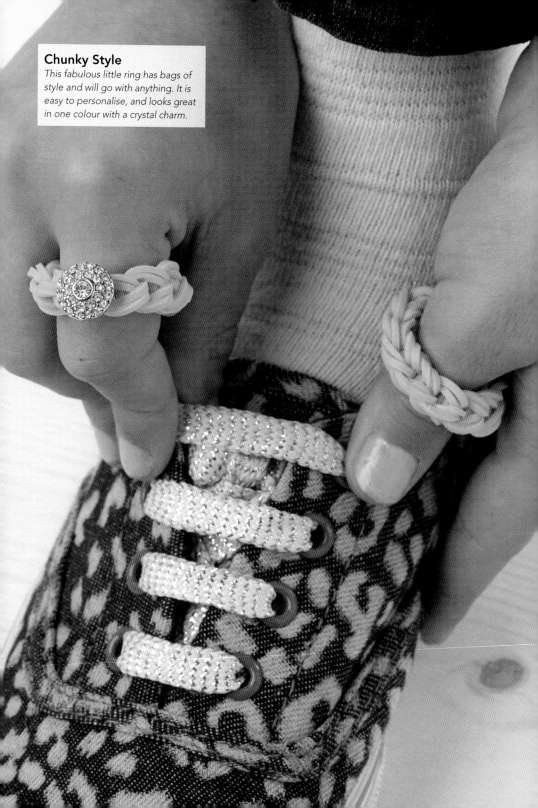

Chunky Style

This fabulous little ring has bags of style and will go with anything. It is easy to personalise, and looks great in one colour with a crystal charm.

Chain Link Necklace ★★★

Materials:

270 x rubber bands (100 x hot pink, 170 x orange)

2 x S-clips

Tools:

Hook

Instructions:

1 This design uses the basic looping technique (see front flap), but you will use two bands to form each loop instead of just one.

2 Fold two orange bands on to the hook and attach an S-clip. Make 29 more double loops. Change to the hot pink bands, and make another 13 loops, then attach another S-clip.

3 Now go back to the first hot pink loop that you made, slide the hook through it, and make 12 loops using the hot pink bands.

4 Slide the hook through the loop that is on the S-clip.

5 Finish the hot pink link by looping a pair of orange bands through the four doubled hot pink loops on the hook, and begin making the second complete link by repeating the same steps as the first hot pink link.

6 Make the third complete link using the hot pink bands.

7 Now make 30 loops using the orange bands and connect the last one to the other end of the S-clip at the beginning of the design to finish the necklace.

Double Decker Bracelet ★★★

Materials:

For the bracelet: 46 x rubber bands (25 x blue, 10 x orange, 10 x yellow, 1 x blue finishing band)

For the extension: 10 x blue bands

1 x S-clip

Tools:

Loom

Hook

Instructions:

1 Adjust the loom, then turn it so the pegs are facing upwards (see page 6). Next, load the loom, following the number sequence in the photograph, right; the outer columns have single blue bands, while the middle column has pairs of one yellow and one orange band.

2 Starting at the bottom, load the first blue band around the middle peg and the peg to its upper left. Load the second blue band from this upper left peg to the one immediately above it, and so on, leaving two empty pegs at the top of the loom.

3 Start at the bottom middle peg again, and this time load a blue band around this peg and the peg to its upper right. Continue loading the bands as you did the left column, leaving two empty pegs at the top of the loom again.

4 Now load the middle column. Load one yellow band from the bottom peg to the one above it. Then load an orange band over the same two pegs. Now load one orange band from the second peg to the one above it; then a second yellow band over the same pegs. Continue in this way until you get to the top three pegs. Then, load two blue bands together over the next pair of pegs, and one single blue band on the last pair of pegs.

5 Turn the loom 180°, so the pegs face downwards.

6 To begin looping, hook the top blue band on the second-from-bottom middle peg, and loop it onto the peg to its upper left. Then hook the other blue band from the same starting peg, looping it to the peg to the upper right.

7 Next, hook the bottom band (blue) on the bottom left peg and loop it to the peg immediately above it. Make sure you push the hook down into the groove to hook the band, not around the outside of the band.

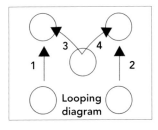

Looping diagram

6

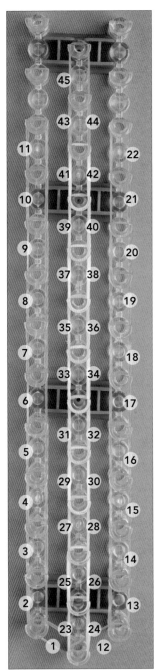

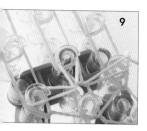

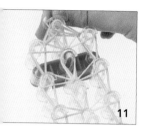

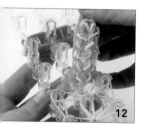

8 Hook the bottom blue band on the bottom right peg and loop it to the peg above it, as in the previous step.

9 From the middle peg third from the bottom, hook the top yellow band and loop it to the upper left peg. Now hook the bottom orange band and loop it to the upper right peg.

10 Now follow the sequence in the Looping diagram (see opposite) until you get to the top of the loom. The blue band on the last left peg (bottom band) is looped to the upper middle peg. Repeat on the right side.

11 Attach a finishing band to all the bands looped around the top peg and make a slip knot (see page 7).

12 Then, starting from the top, gently remove the design from the loom, using the hook to help you. The 'wrong' side faces you as you remove it from the loom.

13 The main design, or 'right' side, is forming on the underside.

14 To extend the bracelet, use the end of the finishing band to make a section using the basic looping technique (see front flap), to whatever length suits your wrist – you will need about 10 bands.

15 Attach an S-clip and connect it to the finishing band at the other end of the bracelet.

Double Value

This bracelet has the added advantage of being reversible. You get a very different effect if you turn it over (see inset image).

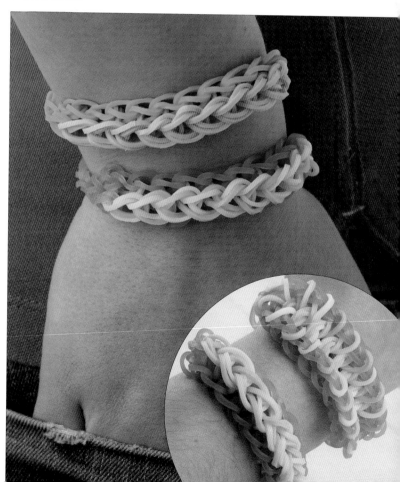

Love Lips Bracelet ★★★

Materials:

45 x rubber bands (16 x orange, 8 x green, 8 x blue, 6 x hot pink, 6 x yellow, 1 x orange finishing band)

1 x black lips button

Tools:

Loom

Hook

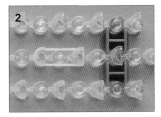

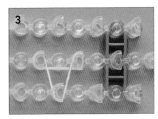

Instructions:

1 Adjust the loom, then turn it so the pegs are facing to the right (see page 6).

2 To load the loom, place an orange band over two pegs on the middle row.

3 Bring the top of the band onto one peg on the row below, so the band is now round three pegs.

4 Add a second orange band on top of this so it forms a triangle shape (this is how you load each band from now on).

5 Now grab the bottom band with the hook and loop it over each peg and into the middle, so that it goes over the top band; it will sit securely in the middle of the three pegs.

6 Continue adding a band and looping the bottom one over the top band and into the middle of the three pegs until all the bands are added. From step 5, add bands in the colour sequence: 2 x green, 2 x blue, 2 x orange, 2 x pink, 2 x yellow (then back to orange). The design will grow quite quickly and the bracelet will emerge from the loom.

7 When you have looped all the bands and your last band is around the peg, finish by hooking the loops on the two top pegs onto the bottom peg. Now transfer the band onto your hook.

8 Thread an orange finishing band through the lips button and pull it through the three loops on the hook.

9 Pull one end of this band through the other.

10 Now loop this end of the band over the button to secure it.

11 Use the loop at the other end of the bracelet to loop over the lips button to fasten it.

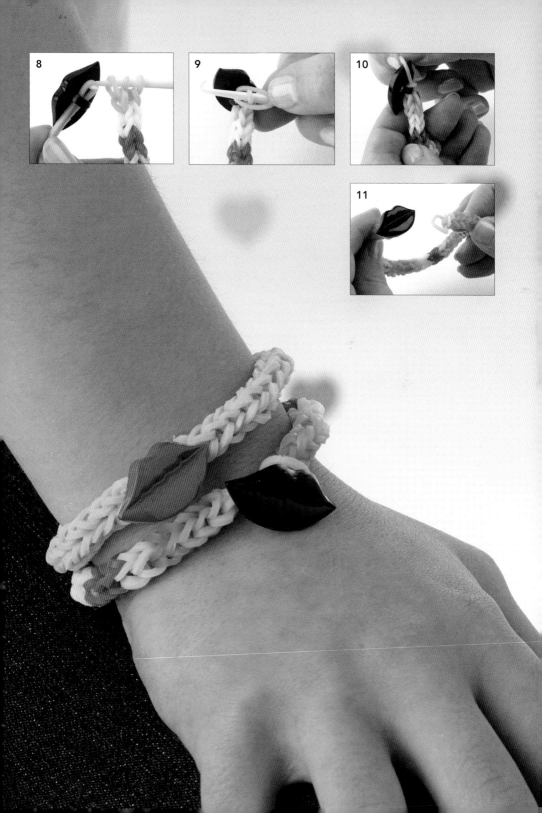

Loop Earrings ★★★

Materials:

64 x rubber bands (14 x green, 12 x orange, 12 x yellow, 12 x blue, 12 x pink, 2 x random coloured bands – hot pink)

2 x silver earwires

Tools:

Loom

Hook

2 x small pair of pliers

Instructions (make 2):

1 Adjust the loom, then turn it so the pegs are facing upwards (see page 6). Load the loom in the same way as you would to make the basic bracelet (see the back flap or follow the number sequence in the photograph, right), but load two bands over each pair of pegs, rather than just one band. Load the bands one at a time, ensuring that they do not twist over each other.

2 Use the following colour scheme – green, orange, yellow, blue, pink – three times, ending with one hot pink finishing band, which will be cut off at the end.

3 Turn the loom 180° so the pegs are facing downwards. You will loop the bands in the same way that you do to make the basic bracelet.

4 Grab the first pair of pink bands with the hook, and loop them from the bottom left peg to the upper middle peg.

5 Continue looping diagonally in this way until you have looped the last pair of green bands onto the top middle peg.

6 Now push the hook all the way through the loops on the last peg and gently remove the whole earring from the loom.

7 Push the hook through the pink bands at the other end, so you now have eight loops on the hook.

8 Pull a new green band through all the loops on the hook, so you now have two green loops on the hook.

9 Finally, attach a silver earwire to the two loops with the pliers, and cut off the random colour band carefully with a pair of scissors.

10 Repeat all the steps to make your second loop earring.

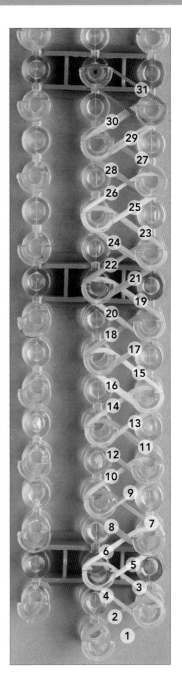

Triple Dipper Bracelet ★★★

Materials:

For the bracelet: 49 x rubber bands
(12 x blue, 18 x yellow, 18 x pink,
1 x blue finishing band)

1 x S-clip

For the extension: 6 x blue bands

Tools:

Loom

Hook

Instructions:

1 Adjust the loom, then turn it so the pegs are facing upwards (see page 6). Load the loom, following the number sequence in the photograph (right). Starting with the left column, load two yellow bands, then two pink bands, and continue alternating between the two colours until you reach the top of the loom. Repeat this process with the middle and right columns.

2 Load the blue bands in a triangle shape, starting at the second middle peg from the bottom, to the top of the loom. Then turn the loom 180°, so the pegs are facing downwards.

3 The looping is also done in three columns. First, hook the bottom left pink band up through the blue band and loop it onto the peg immediately above it.

4 Repeat this with the pink band above it, and so on until you reach the top of the left column. Make sure that you loop the pink and yellow bands up through the blue bands, not around the outside. If you push the hook down into the groove of each peg to grab the band, you should not go wrong. Repeat this process with the middle column, then the right one.

5 At the top of the loom, hook the two loops off the top left peg and transfer them to the top middle peg. Repeat this with the loops on the top right peg, so you now have six loops on the top middle peg.

6 Make a slip knot (see page 7) by taking a blue finishing band and pulling it through all six bands.

7 Pull the end of the band on your index finger over the end on the hook.

8 Then pull the blue band into a knot to secure this end of the bracelet.

9 Starting at the top where the finishing band is, gently remove the bracelet from the loom.

10 Use the end band to add an extension, using the hook and following the basic bracelet pattern (see front flap). Then attach an S-clip, and attach the finishing band to the other side of the S-clip.

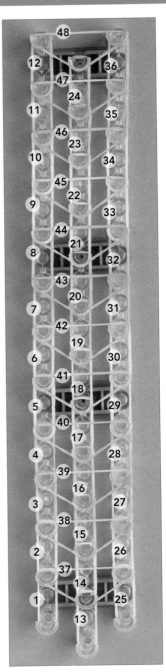

3

4

5

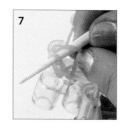

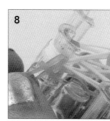

6

7

8

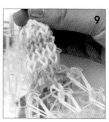

9

Herringbone Bracelet ★★★

Materials:
48 x pink rubber bands
7 x Polaris beads
1 x S-clip

Tools:
Loom
Hook

Instructions:

1 Adjust the loom, then turn it so the pegs are facing to the right (see page 6). This design uses only two pegs in the middle column of the loom. Make a figure of eight (see page 7) with one pink band and place it around the pegs.

2 Then, one at a time, put two further bands on top of this (not as figures of eight this time).

3 If you look at a side elevation of how the bands are loaded on the loom, you can see they form three layers. Make sure that the bands do not overlap each other and that they are not twisted.

4 Starting with the very bottom band, take the left-hand side of the band and loop it over the peg and the top two bands so that it sits in the middle of the two pegs. Now do the same on the right-hand side. Add a new band onto the pegs so you have three layers of bands on the pegs again.

5 Loop the bottom band as before, then add another band. For every six rubber bands, you also add a bead. Beads are added to bands by being threaded on (see page 7 for threading beads onto bands).

6 Once all the bands have been looped, gently remove the design from the loom and attach the two loops onto an S-clip. Then connect the other end of the design to the other side of the S-clip to finish the bracelet.

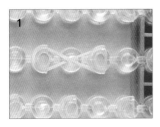
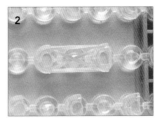

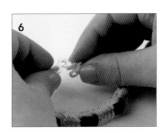

Daisy Chain Bracelet ★★★

Materials:

For the bracelet: 70 x rubber bands
(34 x hot pink, 7 x orange, 7 x pink,
7 x green, 7 x yellow, 7 x blue,
1 x hot pink finishing band)

For the extension: 6 x hot pink
rubber bands

1 x S-clip

Tools:

Loom

Hook

Instructions:

1 Adjust the loom, then turn it so the pegs are facing upwards (see page 6). Load up the loom following the number sequence in the photograph (right). Starting at the bottom middle peg, load one hot pink band from this peg to the upper left peg. Then loop another hot pink band from this peg to the one above, and continue to the top of the loom. Then load the right-hand column in exactly the same way, starting again at the bottom middle peg.

2 Next, load the bands that make the daisies (see order in the loading diagram, below) in the following colour order: orange, pink, green, hot pink, yellow, blue (all bands go from the centre to the side pegs). (If you think of the pegs as a clock face, you load the first band at 2 o'clock, the second at 4 'clock, then 6, 8, 10 and the last one at 12 o'clock.)

3 Work your way up the loom, loading each daisy in turn, as described in Step 2, in the correct colour.

4 The final stage of the loading is to add one doubled band to the centre peg of each daisy, using the same colour band (see page 7 for doubling bands). Finally, add a double-looped hot pink band to the peg at the centre top of the loom (band 69).

5 Turn the loom 180°, so the pegs face downwards. Following the Looping diagram below, start at the bottom middle peg, push the hook into the groove and hook the first blue band below the double-looped band, looping it to the peg immediately above it (in the middle of the daisy).

6 Next, push the hook down into the groove of the centre peg, hooking the band that goes to the bottom right peg, and loop the band over that peg (the same one that it came from).

Looping diagram

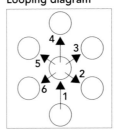

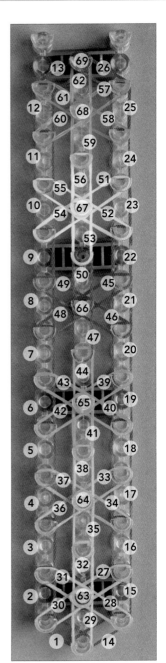

  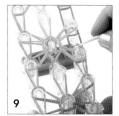 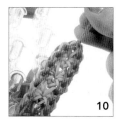

7 Continue looping counterclockwise in this way. The next band is the top right. Once your first flower is complete, go along the loom and loop the rest of the flowers following the looping diagram.

8 Now begin looping the bands on the outside columns. Starting at the bottom middle peg, push the hook into the groove and loop the band second from the bottom and onto the upper left peg it came from. Now hook the bottom band from the peg you just looped to, onto the peg immediately above it. Continue all the way to the top, and finish by looping the top left band to the top middle peg.

9 Return to the bottom middle peg and repeat the looping up the right column in exactly the same way.

10 Secure the bands on the top middle peg with a slip knot (see page 7), using a hot pink finishing band, and gently remove the design from the loom.

11 Connect an S-clip to the finishing band, then add an extension to the other end of the bracelet with the hot pink bands, using the hook and following the basic bracelet instructions (see front flap).

12 Connect the extension to the other end of the S-clip to finish the bracelet.

Pansy Bracelet ★★★

Materials:

For the flower: 20 x rubber bands
(7 x yellow, 6 x pink, 6 x hot
pink, 1 x yellow finishing band

For the bracelet: 21 x rubber
bands (7 x yellow, 7 x hot pink,
and 7 x pink)

1 x S-clip

Tools:

Loom

Hook

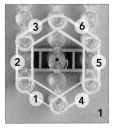

1

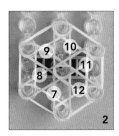

2

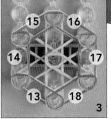

3

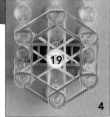

4

Instructions:

1 Adjust the loom, then turn it so the pegs are facing upwards (see page 6). Load the loom in three layers, following the number sequence in the photographs above; starting at the bottom middle peg, load one yellow band to the peg on the upper left, then one band from this peg to the one above it; then one band above that. Go back to the bottom middle peg to load the other three bands counterclockwise.

2 For the second layer, using pink bands, load a band from the middle bottom peg to the one above it (in the centre of the flower shape). Then load the second band from the peg to the lower left to the middle peg. Continue working clockwise until six bands are loaded.

3 For the third layer, start at the bottom middle peg and load the bands in a clockwise direction.

4 Finally, double a yellow band and load it around the centre peg of the flower (band 19).

5 Turn the loom 180° so the pegs are facing down. Push the hook down into the groove of the centre peg (through the double-looped top band) and hook the pink band that goes from this peg to the upper left peg; loop it onto the upper left peg.

6 Continue working counterclockwise in this way, picking up and looping the pink bands from the centre to the peg from which they came.

5

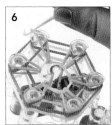

6

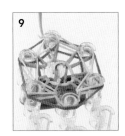

9

10

7 Now push the hook down into the groove of the bottom peg and loop the yellow band that goes from here to the peg to its upper left; loop it onto the upper left peg.

8 Next, loop the yellow band from the upper left peg to the next peg in a clockwise direction, and the one after that.

9 Return to the bottom middle peg and repeat this process counterclockwise to the top peg.

10 Push the hook through the bands remaining on the top middle peg, and secure them with a slip knot (see page 7). Gently remove the pansy from the loom. Keeping hold of both loops carefully undo the slip knot. Push the hook through the loop closest to you, then push the hook through the petals where they cross, then the other loop. Pull the last loop through to create a slip knot.

11 Start off the bracelet just under the edge of the pansy (using the hook and following the basic looping instructions on the front flap), using alternate hot pink, pink and yellow bands. Finish by attaching it neatly to the other underside of the flower using an S-clip.

Bow Headband ★★★

Materials:

21 x blue rubber bands,
   1 x blue finishing band

1 x pink heart button

1 x plastic headband

Tools:

Loom

Hook

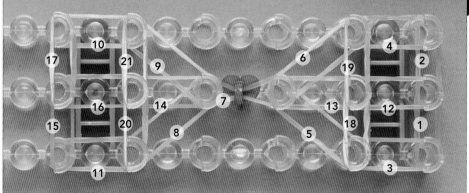

Instructions:

1 Do not adjust the loom – keep it in three rows with the pegs facing towards the left.

2 Load up the loom – please note that bands 17–21 are doubled – following the number sequence above. Make sure when adding the bead in the middle of the design (band 7) that the heart button is facing downwards. When the loom is loaded, you can see that the bands form a bow shape (see above).

3 Turn the loom 180° so the pegs now face towards the right. Follow the instructions using the Looping diagram and the Looping

instructions below. Remember that bands go back to the peg they came from. Take care when going over the doubled bands, as the tension will be tight. Use a finishing band to make a slip knot (see page 7) through all the bands on peg 1. Gently remove the bow from the loom using the hook – taking care not to snap any bands – and pull the finishing band tight to secure it. Reshape the bow.

4 To finish, thread the bow onto a plastic headband using two of the bands on the underside of the bow so that they do not show.

Loop the bands in the following order:

Band 18 to 17
Band 12 to 11
Band 12 to 6
Band 6 to 5
Band 17 to 10
Band 11 to 10
Band 5 to 10
Band 10 to 9 (over the
   heart bead)

Band 9 to 8
Band 9 to 14
Band 9 to 2
Band 14 to 13
Band 8 to 7
Band 2 to 1
Band 13 to 7
Band 7 to 1
Band 1 to finishing band

Looping diagram

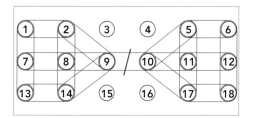

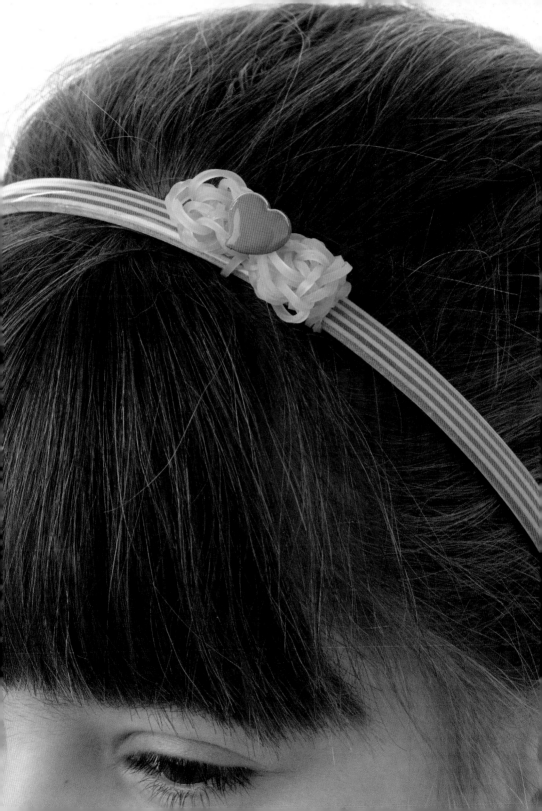

Polaris Bracelet ★★★

Materials:

16 x rubber bands (8 x blue, 8 x pink,
   1 x random colour band)

14 x Polaris beads (7 x blue, 7 x dark pink)

1 x S-clip

Tools:

Loom

Hook

Instructions:

1 Adjust the loom, then turn it so the pegs are facing upwards (see page 6). Load the loom, following the number sequence in the photograph (right); loop a pink band from the bottom middle peg to the one on the upper right of it. A bead is threaded on every band except for the first and last ones; the dark pink beads go on the blue bands and the blue beads go on the pink bands (see right).

2 Load a blue band from the upper right peg diagonally to the one on its upper left. Then load a pink band from this peg out to its upper right. Keep alternating like this until the last band (a blue one), which you load without a bead. Finally, load a random-coloured band (green) from the upper left peg to the upper right.

3 Turn the loom 180°, so the pegs are facing downwards. Ignore the random-coloured band and start looping with the first blue band. Push the hook down into the groove and loop the blue band over the peg and onto the upper left peg.

4 You can see that the band is now looped over the peg from which it came.

5 Next, push the hook into the groove of the same peg and loop the pink band (the band with the first bead), and hook this over the peg to the upper left. This traps the bead within the band.

6 Continue hooking the bands in this way until they are all looped.

7 Attach an S-clip to the top band (pink) and gently remove the design from the loom. Attach the other side of the S-clip to the blue band at the other end of the bracelet and cut off the random-coloured band to complete the bracelet.

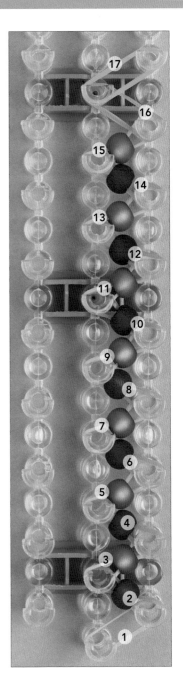

Hairband Heart Charm ★★★

Materials:
33 x blue rubber bands

1 x 40cm length pink lycra cord

Tools:
Loom

Hook

Instructions:

1 Keep the loom as it is, in three straight rows with the pegs facing upwards.

2 Load the loom carefully, starting from the bottom middle peg, and following the numbering sequence in the photograph, right, and the Loading instructions below (please note that some bands are added in twos, some are doubled, and some tripled).

3 Turn the loom 180°, so the pegs are facing downwards.

4 Loop the bands carefully, following the sequence shown in the Looping diagram. Extra care must be taken when looping from pegs 13 and 15, as you need to grab the band below the tripled band. Make a slip knot by threading a finishing band through all the bands on peg 2 and gently remove the design from the loom, taking care not to snap the bands. Straighten out the bands with your fingers and hook so the heart shape looks correct.

5 Attach another band to the top of the heart using a slip knot and thread it onto the length of lycra cord. Tie a knot in the lycra cord to finish the hairband.

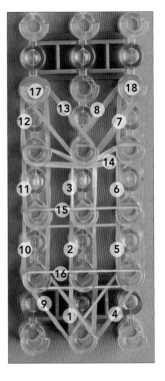

Loading instructions

1 and 2 = 2 bands

3 and 16 = 1 band doubled (band 16 goes over 3 pegs)

4–14 = 2 bands (bands 14 go over the 2 outer pegs and under the centre peg)

14 also goes around the 2 outer pegs and under the middle peg

15 = 1 band over 3 pegs

17 and 18 = 1 band tripled and placed on 1 peg

Special notes

Remember that bands placed on the loom in pairs need to be looped back to the peg they came from. Take care when looping bands *11 to 8, *8 to 5 and *5 to 2, as the tension of the bands is very tight.

Looping diagram

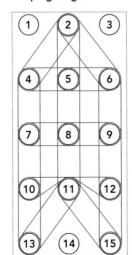

Loop the bands in the following order:

Band 13 to 11 (go into the groove and over the triple band)

Band 13 to 10

Band 10 to 7

Band 7 to 4

Band 4 to 2

Band 15 to 11 (go into the groove and over the triple band)

Band 15 to 12

Band 12 to 9

Band 9 to 6

Band 6 to 2

*Band 11 to 8

*Band 8 to 5

*Band 5 to 2

Band 2 to finishing band

Boodle Bracelet ★★★

Materials:

For the bracelet: 50 x rubber bands
(17 x yellow, 17 x green, 16 x orange)

1 x S-clip

For the extension: 7 rubber bands (3 x
green, 2 x yellow, 2 x orange)

Tools:

Loom

Hook

Instructions:

1 Adjust the loom, then turn it so the pegs are facing upwards (see page 6). Bands are loaded in the colour sequence: 4 x yellow, 4 x orange, 4 x green, except for the first and last bands. Load the loom following the number sequence in the photograph (right); first, load a yellow starting band onto the bottom right peg and the bottom middle peg. Then load bands in squares of four, alternating from one side to the other, as shown right. End with a green band loaded from the top middle peg to the top left peg.

2 Turn the loom 180° so the pegs now face downwards. Then starting at the bottom of the loom, follow the sequence in the Looping diagram below to loop all the bands. Again, this is done in squares of four, similar to the loading sequence. Ignore the first green band and begin looping with the second band. Start with the band on the bottom middle peg that goes to the bottom left peg.

3 Remember to push the hook down into the groove of each peg to grab the band you want, and always loop bands to the peg from which they came.

4 When you have looped the first set of four green bands, you will see a pattern emerging.

5 Continue looping all the way up to the top of the loom.

6 When you reach the top, loop the last band from the top middle peg to the top left peg and attach an S-clip to the bands on the final peg.

7 Gently remove the design from the loom and add an extension using the hook and following the basic bracelet instruction on the front flap.

8 Attach the end of the extension to the other side of the S-clip.

Looping diagram

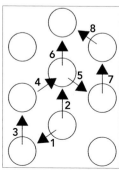

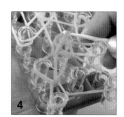

4

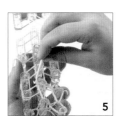

5

6

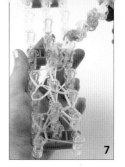

7

Author's note

We hope that you have enjoyed making some of the designs in
this book, or even been inspired to design some rubber band
jewellery of your own. Although the components used in the
designs are widely available, they can all be obtained from the
Beads Direct website: www.beadsdirect.co.uk

The specific components for each project are listed in the
Design Centre on the website, under the name of each piece. If you need
further help or details, please email Beads Direct Customer Service:
service@beadsdirect.co.uk